W9-BME-838

Betsy Ross

by Helen Frost

Consulting Editor: Gail Saunders-Smith, Ph.D.

Consultant: Alan Walden,
Member, Executive Committee,
National Flag Day Foundation

Pebble Books

an imprint of Capstone Press
Mankato, Minnesota

Pebble Books are published by Capstone Press
151 Good Counsel Drive, P.O. Box 669, Mankato, Minnesota 56002
http://www.capstone-press.com

1 2 3 4 5 6 08 07 06 05 04 03

Library of Congress Cataloging-in-Publication Data
Frost, Helen, 1949–
    Betsy Ross/by Helen Frost.
    p. cm. —(Famous Americans)
    Summary: Introduces the life of Betsy Ross, a Philadelphia seamstress who
some people believe sewed the first American flag.
    Includes bibliographical references (p. 23) and index.
    ISBN 0-7368-1641-0 (hardcover)
    1. Ross, Betsy, 1752–1836—Juvenile literature. 2. Revolutionaries—United
States—Biography—Juvenile literature. 3. United States—History—Revolution,
1775–1783—Flags—Juvenile literature. 4. Flags—United States—History—18th
century—Juvenile literature. [1. Ross, Betsy, 1752–1836. 2. Revolutionaries.
3. United States—History—Revolution, 1775–1783. 4. Flags—United States.
5. Women—Biography.] I. Title. II. Series.
E302.6.R77 F76 2003
973.3'092—dc21   2002012513

Note to Parents and Teachers

The Famous Americans series supports national history standards
for units on people and culture. This book describes and illustrates
the life of Betsy Ross. The photographs support early readers in
understanding the text. This book also introduces early readers to
subject-specific vocabulary words, which are defined in the Words
to Know section. Early readers may need assistance to read some
words and to use the Table of Contents, Words to Know, Read
More, Internet Sites, and Index/Word List sections of the book.

Table of Contents

Elizabeth Griscom was born in Philadelphia on January 1, 1752. Her family called her Betsy. She had 16 brothers and sisters.

historic Society Hill in Philadelphia

6

Betsy learned to sew
at home and at school.
She made clothes and
quilts for her family.

a young girl learning to sew

8

Betsy stopped going to school at age 12.
She became an apprentice at a sewing shop.

a sewing shop in the 1700s

Betsy married John Ross in 1773. John and Betsy opened a sewing shop. John died two years later. Betsy kept the shop open by herself.

Betsy sewed clothing
in her shop. She also
made covers for furniture.

a young woman sewing

In 1776, the United States was becoming a new country. It did not have a flag. Some people think that Betsy helped design and sew a flag for the new country.

In 1777, the Continental Congress chose a national flag. Some people believe it was like the flag that Betsy made.

the design of the first flag of the United States

18

Betsy got married two more
times after John died.
She had seven daughters
and many grandchildren.
She told them stories
about her life.

Betsy died in 1836.

Her grandson began to tell

the story about Betsy

making the first flag.

This may be how the legend

of Betsy Ross sewing the

first American flag started.

Words to Know

apprentice—someone who learns a trade or a craft by working with a skilled person

Continental Congress—the group of leaders who made laws for the American colonies before they became the United States of America

flag—a piece of cloth with a pattern that is a symbol of a country, state, or organization; the first United States flag had seven red stripes and six white stripes; the flag also had 13 stars that formed a circle on a blue square in the upper left-hand corner.

legend—a story handed down from earlier times

quilt—a warm, usually padded, covering for a bed; many quilts are made of pieces of cloth sewn together in a pattern.

sew—to make, repair, or fasten something with stitches made by a needle and thread